FIRST TIME, EVERY TIME

FIRST TIME, EVERY TIME

Lisa Titus

Brick Road Poetry Press
www.brickroadpoetrypress.com

Copyright © 2023 by Lisa Titus

Cover art: photo © 2023 by Anne Marchal; cover design © 2023 by Jeff Prybolsky
Author photo: © 2023 Jeff Prybolsky

Library of Congress Number: 2023944790
ISBN: 978-1-950739-11-0

Published by Brick Road Poetry Press
341 Lee Road 553
Phenix City, AL 36867
www.brickroadpoetrypress.com

Brick Road logo by Dwight New

ALL RIGHTS RESERVED
Printed in the United States of America

For the women who made me and for my fierce, magical daughter

Table of Contents

I

Midnight Hives..3
Lost Art...4
When Not Hungry, Restless..5
Over Shots of Tequila You Ask Me What My Bee Poem Means and Why I Always Push You Off the Cliff in Your Dreams............................6
Birth Song...7
So The Story Goes..8
Vision..9
My Son Asks Me If Witches Are Cold-Blooded..............................10
Night Fishing...11
Things I Tell My Children..12
February..13
Ars Poetica..14
Things I Don't Tell My Children..15
Sons of Phaeton..16

II

God's Reply...19
Even gods..20
What We Believe...21
Eve's First Party..22
Between Worlds..23
Suspension of Disbelief...24
The Dangers of Thimbles (Or Giving Out Kisses).........................25
Ophelia Rising...26
Fairytale..27
How It Really Happened...28
Before the Bite..29
Predetermined..30
I Don't Know What Love Is...31

III

After Ever...35
Confessions...36
A Woman Wants to Make Love to a Poet.......................37
All In...38
Clarity...39
Ride It Out...40
No Joke...41
Breaking In..42
I'm Sure You Were Handsome..43
Camouflage..44
What You Came For..45
Morning Light..46
Desire..47
Lost Men..48

IV

On Being Grown-Up...51
The Trick...52
This Ruined World..53
Philter...54
Summer Night..55
Don't Take My Advice..56
These Days..57
Early Spring, Sullivan County, NY.................................58
When Sadness Comes...59
Slipstream..60
What the Truth is Worth..61
It's best, you say, if you keep that opinion between us......62
Trash Talk..63
These Boots Were Made...64
Re-Vision...65
The River Knows...66
Circus Life...67
Our Only Escape..68
Small Town Prayers..69
August Light...70

"Like the dead-seeming cold rocks, I have memories within that came out of the material that went to make me."

—Zora Neale Hurston

"…I grew up
according to legend,
but only a little."

—Kim Addonizio, "Eulogy"

I

Midnight Hives

The harvest moon is six hours late
and I can't catch up. Houses, fences,
cars dive into the dark like wrecked ships.
I gain my bearings — shadows move
through the field, corrupt ghosts
whose dirty hands drag the grass —
and listen for the hum of the bees.

Weeks I refused to be led here,
Boundless apprehension fueled excuses:
I fear the dark, the lumbering bears, the
abrupt silence of crickets like a pinprick,
blood rising to the surface of midnight.

I am told to close my eyes and walk; he strides
ahead, a drunk man bitten sober,
no stumbling over tree roots or rotting branches.
I map the distance to the outline of boxes,
greedy for the whirring I'd predicted and recognize
as soon as I am close enough: it is a life,
or death, an alien motor, a moon engine.

He demands I come closer, *just smell them,
they won't sting you, they know I am here.*
He is leaning down, his ear to a box, talking
to me, to the queen, his prayer thickening
their universe, but I can't hear him —
they are droning in my head
like an incantation heard centuries ago —

I am shedding the moonlight, drinking the shadows,
rooting, growing, branching yellow flower heads,
smelling of earthy orgies,
feral and alive like the hot breath of birth:
the goldenrod, the bees.

Lost Art

At three a.m. I stand in an uncertain shed
breathing thick, heavy heat. The drunk man
I drove here after the bar closed pulls frames
of honeycomb out of boxes, identifies the type —
clover, citrus, basswood deep as roots.
My fingers press into comb after he rakes off wax;
honey weeps like amber sweat, primordial ooze
of natural selection and methodical habits learned,
bad decisions licked from fingertips dirty with an afterthought
of midnights past where bare lightbulbs and turned down
eyes lit the best way home.

Buckets of sweetness stand in the way of the door
but he is talking about bees, his humming connection to a universe
so complete that any other perfection is a joke — people
are too easy to figure out. I am only a bystander, though useful,
as there are universes to be transferred like hives loaded onto pick-up trucks.
This universe is dripping like moonlight down tree branches,
slow and syrupy like drunk dancing on hardwood floors with weepy
knots, slick and silent as the arms of a lead with steel-toed boots.
Half dead bees stumble onto his fingers. I am alarmed by his violent flick,
the bees lit on their own power and how it will kill them. Everything is sticky
like closed mouths and ransacked desire. I walk back
into the darkness, dispose of my pollen, drink the deep gold
of this universe, one I can find
on my own.

When Not Hungry, Restless

The last slider of autumn
hums past lazier than usual
like crawling honey bees
picking their way through flowerless
lawns, prepared for their winter cluster.

We, we are no longer
bee-drunk on air. Pollen settles
into the creases of faces, fingers'
callouses fade. Last season's uniform benched,
a tanner version of you ghosts about,

seeks a sliver of sun. You shield your eyes
with your glove and squint, I turn and turn
untethered while Mercury does laps.
Falling backwards, sleepless stones
shiver frequencies tuned to loss.

Don't ask how stars communicate.
If I miss your slouched grin, your lazy lean
over the bar, your eyes latched globes
hiding a snowless winter, a blue deepened
by melting, but no longer want to unhook them,

can I still call it desire?
This longing will not sleep. Listen carefully
as you hold this match to the hive, I whir within
this winter, a million fastballs, perfect spinning planets.
Sustained by a golden drug, I'm ready

for the tilt of the earth to summon
the sun, for the first pitch
of spring to sing its way through the dark,
the first crocus tempting me
to eat whatever you offer.

Over Shots of Tequila You Ask Me What My Bee Poem Means and Why I Always Push You Off the Cliff in Your Dreams

In warm October, the bees still crawl through lavender,
hover over goldenrod, staging a fall
masquerade, signaling the sober girl
who mourns the crushed universe,
the pollen of my tears feeding a new loss
on repeat — the green baked to brown,
milky sunlight transformed to honey,
the work of creatures searching the thistle
and clover for one last sip.

If I drink enough, I can explain the breakdown
of our evolution, how I was not meant to cry
into a morning cup, roll the stones
of my discontent all day to earn enough
to carry the heavy weight of breath.
If I put down this shot glass,
drag you to the mountain's edge where
sky gives way to meadows still raving with color,
you will hear the electric hum of this world, the rot
and light of bold magic, the sting of knowing
and how we lost it. Do we have to fall
to remember how to live? Or can we

reach for roots, burrow into the bones
of soil to sleep dreamless, drunk
on the bees droning deep into their night.
We could remember who we are, the foggy-eyed,
violet winter would not seem so foreign
as the winged ancestors of birth
and death cycle us through another season,
hold us steady with their song.

Birth Song

Inside us black birds sing, beaks poking holes in the belly
of my hurt and yours and ours. Scars carried like jewels,
talons wrap around a world we want to save
while it drowns in animal blood. We saw this coming,

metal traps gleam like all things
coveted just before dark, like hooded blasphemy, like a woman's
open thighs, shadows flooding a briny plague. So we push forward,
reach out of a warm womb towards a mother we could kill,
kill for, pray it will be different this time.

Just yesterday, I saw an old woman pull a black feather
from her mouth, words running like hooves in sand,
trying to heal a crying child with spells. The child peered
at the feather through the light of a shedding sun,
the child preened then swallowed the feather,
smiled at the winged silence
in the old woman's eyes,
the weight of a new world filling her belly.

So The Story Goes

For Ron

When I told him I was a shapeshifter,
he was not surprised. He had known
women like me — mother, sisters, wives
with wolves' teeth for blood, owl's talons
for eyes. Most men don't believe

what they have when they have us
so we ghost through their houses, leave webs
in their beds. We are not elegant,
whimsical; vapor trailing up mountainsides,
courtesans sighing through closed doorways.
We walk heavily, sip whiskey, hang laundry
over lattice, trace naked bodies
in sleep, wake with them crumpled
beside us, grizzled and rare. His dark stare

hung quietly over the bar. He brought small gifts,
asked for only conversation, my loud laugh,
held my shapes like a secret, his hands hardened
by iron-work folded on the counter,
wise from his ancestor's lore that warned
this magic is real — women like me disappear
the moment you build the pedestal. Foolish

in our youth, we wished to marry the stars
but in spite of the tale, didn't miss the earth;
we return to pour scotch on the rocks,
guard paintings of the night sky — we are pathfinders,
stiletto-stompers, rain-keepers — certain men
find us, palm open our wild, taste our skin
on their shadows, believe.

Vision

Somewhere between the Catskills and Buffalo
I am driving too fast. My infant son waits for me
to come home to rock him to sleep while my mother
dozes in a hospital bed, puffy and achy
from surgery. My world is a blur,

like my lenses are the wrong prescription, like I am flying,
eyes open, through a tornado. Why weren't we born
with wings? Why didn't some god borrow feathers
from hawks or seagulls, sew them
to our shoulders, give us perspective? I can't see

past the last 24 hours of my life — the waiting room,
the phone in the corner and its sudden startle, shaking fingers
snatching it off the hook. Family members pace, joke
through crossword puzzles, try not to find
"lymph nodes" or "colon" in the coded words, deny

silent dangers that snake through our
lives. People in cars I fly past have mothers
calmly folding laundry right now, or strolling in a park,
reaching back to rub an aching shoulder, maybe stopping
to look around.

My Son Asks Me If Witches Are Cold-Blooded

I pull out my bones so he can throw them, read his history. I sweep swamps, woods for roots to make broth. I tame the bees who sting me, draw honey from the wounds. I pierce my lips with blackberry briars, press them to his forehead. I feed him from my bowl, warm his hand in mine.

Night Fishing

The improbability that fish
larger than dreams could live
in an ankle-deep stream
was what troubled us most.
Not that our children

could hold their breath,
scoop the monsters
into their arms, press them
to bursting chests, gills pulsing,
tails thrashing, suffocating
from joy or pain — we could only guess
what they have known —

and haul them to us, smiling
with inhaled anticipation —
a distant memory of survival
nets them, trembles
through us.

Things I Tell My Children

Always carry a dark stone, a mute bluebird, a sharp arrow, homing devices nobody questions. Trust animals — human directions are deceitful, their bones lie (love them anyway). Share your poems whenever possible, only sacrifice survives, map the consequences with metaphor; the poem is always truth. A dewdrop cannot be saved, let it dry so the stars have a trail to follow, feed the deer fermented apples, they may stumble, steady; the skies' reflection in their eyes is a prayer — say it. Look a loved one dead in the face, blame your defiance on your mother, her damp hands feeding earth soft men, when briars grab your legs as you run, bloody scratches become new words (the stinging eventually subsides): write them. Listen to the fish dreaming at lake's bottom, swallow the weight of the stone in your pocket, be silent, the birch branches all sway in the right direction, look up. Be grateful — your arrow points to verses the startled bluebird sings once you give her voice.

February

My daughter was born on the fifth day,
an afterhours blood-letting that freckled
my face with rioting red capillaries. She,

she came with a yawning stronger than
hipbones, a rasp of oak leaves
tearing across a field of ice, leaving daggers.

She bled first on the nineteenth,
first full moon after her twelfth birthday,
a super snow moon, the wolves' howling dead

in their throats, heads turning away from
shining to behold a mother they could worship.
She is not the storm, she doesn't even know

the storm is coming, her sticky thighs
only an inconvenience, a change of clothes
easily avoided if womanhood

held her horses, pulled up on those wild
mares a little harder. My daughter showed her teeth,
her spine of arched fingernails, her body

a forest of questions she asks without rest:
*What will I be? Who will I conquer? Why
do you cry?* And I wipe my eyes with her

hair, recite the kind of prayer unheard by gods
as she harnesses these winds, horses she will spur
through flurries, blizzards nobody will see coming.

Ars Poetica

At forty-three, a mother
of afghan patterns and sheer drapery,
I have nothing to hide. These hands,
heavy with forgiveness and cracked
knuckles, know no other way to knit
my story, drunken primroses stitched
through fields, howling at everybody else's sun.

It is bright today; mid-March
promises I will teethe soon,
send my splintering hallelujahs spiraling
through the next cruel month. Bloody
as blooming I smile into the light
wearing lunatic's clothes, or maybe naked
because this is how babies are born:
everybody runs towards the cries,
hushes the distracted horror circling
another body. Spring mutinies, tubers
find new arrangements, tangle and tear.
I want just a little cover, wool to warm
my roots as I unknot and stretch,
needles click, weave this yarn into a shroud
I'll be unburied in.

Things I Don't Tell My Children

I. Son

Before you were born, my dreams
were oceans swallowing me, I harbored a gutted
womb awash in awful silences. To drown
was to escape the holiness I was chasing.
A fear of water overwhelmed me when I held you,
a new mercy I had to save from the sucking
black depths, a frail craft capsized, then righted.
Panic when bathing you rose in me; a red tide washing
gilled monsters onto the beach breathing, threatened
to carry you to the deep end, forced me to crawl
from the bathroom, a slippery life
in my arms.

II. Daughter

You were born from an ocean well, drawn
from the damage of deep sighs. A bright baptism
of salt water sang you into being. Your cries
woke me before you were born, I counted
your tears into rivers that fed countries I never
wanted to visit. As an infant, you slept beside me
on a rickety raft fashioned from flower stems and lily pads;
I dreamed of losing you through gaps
in my heartbeat. I held you; floods of peripheral
scum terrorized me. Nothing was safe enough:
that pond we drove by daily could lure my car,
a slick eel sliding us in, buckles failing as we sink,
water expectant between us: I could never hold you
this close again.

Sons of Phaeton

Early spring basketball courts
teem with shirtless teenage boys;
steeds of Helios, rippling with the marrow
of gods and dangerous decisions.
The ball flies between them, their skill
an art newly discovered like arrogance.
Their game ends with shouts,
exhaled snorts and mumbled curses
shroud the evening pinks.
They trot steady from the hoops,
smoke of grey light sifts behind them,
the sun bowing low ahead. Eyes like flames
untended, they're not strong enough
to rein in the world,
but able to set it ablaze.

II

God's Reply

Your words are inaudible,
a foreign language with no translation.
I concentrate on eel and violet,
beetle and willow reed,
their tongue-less silence soothes.
Where did you hide your children?
I hear them breathing
through locked doors;
Strain to hear their voices,
tiny music boxes
filtering through the air
like alarmed chickadees,
their blood giddy —
but they are stricken
oceans lapping at my feet.
I am swallowed
by injured whales, galaxies
hiding inside them
a welcomed static.

These razed fields
sleep in my lungs
like held breath, dandelion
ash paves my throat.
Surrounded by burning bushes,
angry fires singe my eyebrows,
the smoke an acrid prayer.
My hands cannot hold
these sorrows, these pulverized
hymns whisper through my fingers,
tingling stars poke holes
in my only escape.
There is no peace here;
knees ache from concrete bruises,
a shotgun nuzzles my temple,
a world I didn't create
bellows in my ears.

Even gods

Even gods hunger
Sometimes; mouths agape, empty
Beasts who shotgun
The first riotous feast offered.
Even gods wake from dreams
Peopled with the lost, ghosts
Handing out fistfuls of dusk,
Unable to tell one world from the other,
Thirsty and panting. They dribble
Wine down blouses, drop cocktail
Glasses at gatherings, cry on the porches
Of strangers cursing their gasoline lies.
They slam screen doors, avoid people they know
In grocery stores, break promises. Even

gods wander into hushed rooms
Before realizing they don't belong, slink
Back into the night, bum a cigarette,
Drive fast to outrun regret.
They grip the slick waist of the steering wheel
Like first loves who encouraged them
To brake hard on the bridge,
Climb up on the railing,
Body swaying with mortal thrill
In the fuzz of headlights, arms full of sky.

What We Believe

We make offerings to unseen gods;
ripped bandage of scarred skin, broken urn
of forgotten ashes, molded penny of fathomless fortunes,
eyes turned up or down, filmy with belief.
This is what we've learned: ache briefly for faith
and it will appear, all flashing lights and swirling feathers
swooping us into a down comfort of bliss.

But you ignite or drown for less: a flash of sunlit eyes,
sweet lilt of voice, wry curve of a question smirking
with the hope of *maybe*. You wade deep into dark
water, gingerly toeing grainy truths, led by a moist
hand, light friction of fingertips a fragile promise:
Hold your breath, love, this will only take a moment.

Or, you streak through the flame like a dancing star,
eyes open, flailing and singeing, a crackling brightness,
a song you've never heard before rising from your throat —

Oh, god. I burn for you.

Eve's First Party

Look at her: cider-drunk and wistful
as an orchard keeper in midday sun
squinting beyond rows of twisted branches
for a glimpse of a god who forgives
small fuck-ups: rotten fruit and Friday's tragedies
rewound and examined, replayed on Sunday
after the service, after all has been written.

        She committed every sin
        to memory, soaked them in vinegar to preserve
        potency: the first time a dare was hissed
        in her ear and she took it in her mouth,
        savored the pink honey of the lie, the last
        time she kissed a man, his wilderness spread
        before her like a garden she would never eat from.

Years, she hovered at the forest's edge,
lonely in a forever planned out by someone
who never showed his face privately,
who avoided her birth-cries, her mud bruises.
The heat of earth protected her from plagues and pictures,
the quiet shadow of her flesh a hidden door
now swung open, now torn off its hinges.

        Uninvited, she slithers through guests' shocked
        silence, a snake awakened in a winter grove.
        She sways toward him, direct and precise,
        like a bite, teeth sour in the wake
        of her smile, red smear of lips steal
        the eyes of every man and demigod she shimmies past,
        a quiver below the belt buckling their knees.

She does not apologize as expected, meets
his eyes, globes still as marbles mid-spin,
nail holes in his hands spilling seeds,
drink suspended just below an open mouth.
He reaches for her, folds his body into a prayer,
a god who has seen his own image, past mistake
confirmed by the miracle; pale pink blossoms
of her story, blood-scorched and flickering,
bloom in his hand.

Between Worlds

Dogs are howling up and down my block,
                       but it's not my fault: I worship the sun. I am a traitor
to my sex,
      my gender,
my sex.
           I'll change my name.
                   Dear Hades:
                   What did Persephone do
                      all those days in the dark? Did she sew by firelight?
                      Could she even dance in cloistered shadows?
No. She must've danced in the firelight,
                                       in the fire,
her dress a singed rainbow, her hair sun-spent daffodils,
         skin unlicked. She is every fire the summer
summoned heat for, every letter of a love poem sifted through air
         like pollen. She spins; words into luster, daybreak on the surface of
an accidental mirror, kindling craving drought, ignited,
         draped in a grieving hood like mothers torching days and nights for lost
            daughters.
                               Helios help them.
               To hell
     with your perspective.
We drift between worlds, shed petals of ashes,
          a smokescreen of whispers you can choke on in broad daylight, pome-
           granate trees
swaying in our wake, and — damn-it — we love.
                        We get back to where we belong.

Suspension of Disbelief

I am the tree limb blocking the road
after a storm — stubborn and heavy god —
Monday night whiskey breath ignored
on Tuesday morning. I am a broken pod,

seeds feathering out, settling on an eyelash,
a pine needle; hollyhock grown too tall
dragged down by flower heads to kiss thick gash
of dirt. I am a crow's gifts; small

gems, omens, strings knotted, cut, ransomed
for all that's held in your arms, then replaced.
I am the perfect starling's nest abandoned,
wisp of spider's web settled across your face,

white dress whispering through your dreams,
lace caught between your fingers, then released.

The Dangers of Thimbles (Or Giving Out Kisses)

When you came to me that night
and told me I could fly,
I wanted to believe you; the gold dust
of my youth settled over your lies.

Now, I stand at the window whispering
words to a song long dead,
the second star on the right winking
me far into morning.

The lost men gather at my skirts,
saddling the guilt of my sins —
little boys' fists clutch my hemline
with their refusal to grow. Oh, I wish

I had been strong enough to shove you
back into the night. I wish the stars
would have prophesied the danger of saving
like they foretold the lines on my face.

I would have known, all this time,
just how old I would grow.

Ophelia Rising

When I rose, dripping from the river,
I had forgotten everything; sky and water
met in godless communion. The violets
are wilted yet blaze a purple-flamed
craving. Where are the willow boughs
that promised to hold me? And why did the dream
of a man's love lead to the deepness
of a grave? I would rather be secured
by a brothel's strong walls where velvet whispers
kiss my ear, drown the sorrow of remembering.
I want nothing more than to run to my mother's arms
where the hum of death can reach me. I want nothing:
the silence of a convent, that brutal hush
that pushes madness back into the dark
well from which it came.

Fairytale

In another life, my grandmother didn't take any shit, drank beer only from frosty mugs, lit cigarettes with burning coals. When she spoke, the warm growl rose from her belly like a weapon, like her fur might stand on end, might prickle if you touched. In this life,

she still supervised a toy factory, her workers still spoke of her with winged breathlessness. She still laughed with the graveled choke of a tractor engine, still let the sun tell her what to do. In this life, nobody turned away from her secrets, we felt the whole height

of her five-feet-eight-inch frame like you feel the shadow of an apple tree, the healed bark of one who has born, who will bear again, the fruit that fills us as we bloom then ripen, limbs draped with the fullness of birth and death, gifts dropping as we ferment at her feet.

In this life, the wasps made nests in the hollow trunk, not in her brain. In this life my grandmother buried the wolves of her past in a shallow grave marked with a spent 45 Long Colt. The last animal to assume the pale white of her neck was weakness knew too well: he bowed low when she walked by, she wore his teeth around her neck.

How It Really Happened

The darkness became an ache so she cupped stars in her hands
like fireflies, an easy light filling a universe created
from galaxies of immortal refuse: recycled thighs, the smoothness
of muscle and bone, layers of hair dug from bins behind the last
silent four billion years. She braided it together,
new wind of her breath lifted it like the silky strands of inchworms.

There were no violent explosions, no choking dust or meteoric fireworks,
she just parted the fog of confused gases, held her breath.
A somber parade of new visions emerged: jellyfish blinking into
muskrats, small whispers of snakes parting grass,
a droopy-eyed teenage boy reaching for the sweet fruit
held just out of reach.

Unfiltered light created waves that gently lipped shores
giving birth to the first sound, her own sigh, a vast flutter of blackbirds
rising to the surface, dipping their wings in sky, the fiery red glinting
like the sun's reflection in a mirror where she does not look for herself,
mesmerized by the bright moon dangling over a garden she planted, the soil
still darkening her fingernails as she reached for the beginning where
there were always stars, not this blaze of knowing, this mushy apple
falling from her hand.

Before The Bite

She talked him into marrying
At Niagara Falls, the Canadian side,
Before they gambled away
Their sins and blessings. This distasteful
Match hidden for some time —
God's attention hijacked
By rainbow colors and ostrich feathers.
They skipped the promises
And got right to the celebration.
There was wine, of course,
The cheap kind in glass jugs,
And a dainty appetizer or two
Inviting the ravenous hunger
That results in precarious situations
Like his head in her lap
At the train station, the whistle
Distracting, a warning hissed in his ear
Over the sharp teeth of a migraine,
the sun bleeding over the waterfall.
The market vendors unpacked
Crates of fall fruit, apples
Shiny as the red corvette across
The street, driver winking in the rearview,
Her face suddenly flushed,
Fingers grip flesh, her husband's arm
Fresh bruised, the apple's skin tingles
exposing the mistake she made,
the scaled underbelly of choice.

Predetermined

She didn't even like apples
But accepted his gift,
Carried twelve children including
The baby born blue, a bruise
Never faded. Nothing happened
Like she pictured: not the canopied
Bed, windchimes in the trees,
Birds singing at the window,
An un-poisoned promise poised
Like a desperate unknowing.
As a child she hated sweets;
The treats distant uncles brought
Trapped her hands and mouth
In heavy stickiness. She didn't like
Dirt, either, but here she is knuckle-deep
In soil, raw fingertips digging deeper
Into her memory for where she buried
That offering, the snakeskin purse
Hidden under wooden floorboards,
Trinkets of a life lacking hunger
And twenty-two eyes asking always
For too much. She imagines the ivory
Of the piano keys beneath her hands,
Hums the old songs the uncles
Sang, her tongue tingling with the bite
Of crisp, white flesh. No sudden hush,
A flock of birds sweeping the clouds outside,
She squints, searches the horizon for a savior,
For a sign; trees out past the field, blighted
Fruit dangling for all but her
To take.

I Don't Know What Love Is

I don't know what love is but I know when it
            gathers in me,
                      shuffles through the dusty church like a Lost Congregation,
      a holy note
etched into their tongues, shards of stained glass held in their mouths
like an offering — Mother-blue light,
                      a jagged hymn cupping the white psalm of her son.
       Lovers kneel beneath him
unable to blot the stains of small mercies from their hands, their feet.
                        I swallow the sweet wine of promise as your voice rises,
            filling
chinks in this clapboard heart, lifting me from a crumbled foundation to stand
    twisted,
       hands clasped tightly, this holy ghost caught between them, an orange globe
pulsing,
             emitting a light like fire in empty pews.
                                That one song settles in the back of my
                    throat.

III

After Ever

When you pulled the dead girl from the river,
Wiped the muck from her sightless eyes,
Slicked the hair back from her forehead,
She stirred slightly, aware of a power in your hands
She might call tenderness had she ever known it.

For years she waited for her killers to be erased,
They hung so long from the rope
Of her pain, hope threadbare as the dress
Clinging to her body like seaweed.

You are not a princess, you said, and she shivered
Because this new life is as real as your fingers
Unhooking her, the water rushing clear
From her mouth.

Confessions

Does it matter where it happened? Does it matter middle of a farmer's field NY/ UB frat house bathroom/ behind the Old Main Inn after closing? Does it matter a boy saved me after the weight of two held me down/ jager-bomb heavy/ ten quarter drafts heavy/ last time this happened nobody was around heavy? Does it matter my roommates left me at that party singing "It's More Than A Feeling" cross-legged on a mattress/ two boys stoned slug-eyed squishing closer? If I turn around quickly enough will I remember that boy's name/ catch his hand leaving the next morning/ thank him for throwing his body across mine to protect me from his friends? If I put down my beer before I go into the bathroom which girl will guard it for me? Will she roll her eyes or smile when I come back? Will she laugh with her dude-friends the day after they pin me to the wall lather me with beer foam lips/ drag fingers over my breasts stomach legs? How will I get home at 3 am with a head full of no's and one more shot to make the shame thinner easier to swallow? *Hey bro you got a blanket? I'll even take your t-shirt/ please tell me where my clothes are/ I'll walk back to the dorms/* remember you locked me outside your room kept my bra as a souvenir? I laughed it off avoided your homies for weeks/ does it matter if it happened 25 years ago/ 17 years ago/ 3 years ago/ 225 days ago?

America, I am the slut you heard about (don't worry, I never told; I'll still fuck you dizzy). I am the shadow bird warning, a swarm of one funneling dark rage into the morning-after air. I will unzip your secret conquests — your guilt spilled, a public gasp, into the collective truth. Your boys are not safe from their own hands, their own ungoverned bodies. I will expose empty parking lots, back bedrooms where nobody asked questions worth asking. I will fly into your mouths all smoke and charred smiles. I will hock my truths. I've nothing left
to fear.

A Woman Wants to Make Love to a Poet

Hopefully, before the moment of waking,
when dreams weaken, he will be gone.
She does not expect he will be penning his tribute
to her near a dawn-lit window. Romance isn't

the half of it – she knows desire, those
untrimmed claws tearing at the cushions
of her guts. She knows how to nurse
the weeping scars, so she doesn't need
tenderness, either. She doesn't know how to listen
to the soil, doesn't know why
she is saddened by dry riverbeds
and acres of unplanted ploughed fields.

She's not speaking to the shopowners, turning
keys in locks for the night, and is angry
At the young boys kicking stones across the street
who doze in their beds at night, not hearing
the purr of a spinning earth and will never brim
with wonder when touching a woman.

She imagines Neruda eating fruit in an orchard
decayed, feels cummings' hands measuring
the rain, peers at Whitman through parted curtains
and tries to go to each man, hold him like an image
imbedded in broken glass, longs to
take the world inside of her and make it shudder.

All In

We were suffocating near the water
a rock beneath us when we first kissed,
the moments beforehand awkward
like bubbles painfully breathing from the bottom
of the lake escaping the intense pressure
of deepness. When you finally pressed your lips to mine,
the relief was so furious the only way to absorb it
was to grasp your hand, touch your face, sink into eyes
that revealed you weren't anchored either.
Even the solid surface beneath us was melting,
and to net the slippery monsters swimming
in the pool of our feelings, we pulled back hard.
The only way to breathe underwater is to adapt.
So there was only one thing to do:
Drown.

Clarity

This is a poem that admits I see clearly
past truths that make sense to me now.
I don't regret things I've said insincerely —

we all have to find our own meaning — nearly
forsaking gods and breath in a rush of vows
we finally write down after seeing. Clearly

certain things were true. In the past, through bleary
vision we construct monuments to hopes we sow,
then lament lost art, blame the creator for insincerely

guiding us in the wrong direction; for (dear me!)
not providing us with the proper tools. We allow
poems written to things not seen clearly

because we fear losing. I remember gingerly
freeing my lips from yours; I didn't understand how
you could be so indecisive about love, sincerely

admitting the lack of clarity in a kiss. Eerily
struck with a similar notion, irony clinches crowds
of poems written by those who see clearly;
I don't regret truths spoken insincerely.

Ride It Out

I am the rusty razor jabbed into your ribs, the saw with no teeth, grinning. I am the rope burning your wrists and ankles, the voice whispering in your ear: *You did this to yourself my pretty, my life, my word of god,* sneaking through cracked lips, sticking to a swollen tongue. I am the black and white villain clapping like a delighted child, the piano music tumbling through the air as the train smokes into sight. I am the good luck penny placed on the twisted track, the one rotted tie; the empty space, empty space, empty space between panic and bliss.

No Joke

A guy walks into a bar, a guitar strapped
To his back. The young girls in khaki jumpsuits swoon.
His arms are mapped with stories, his eyes lucky pennies.
You roll your eyes — you've heard this one before.

You make him a gin, the bar tilts towards him. He plays
a song you vaguely remember, it stings like lime juice
in finger cuts. You shrug, pour another drink, shoulders stuck
by your ears, chest a cavern of trapped breath.

He sings a story from a dream that once startled you awake,
breathless, swooping bats thrash against your ribs.
You hug yourself, massage your aching sides,
hope his voice will drown

in the soapy sink, that the drain will not clog
with his words left swirling in your mouth.
You refill his drink, resist the urge to rub the melody
from his calloused fingers, keep it from getting you drunk.

But it's too late: you're smashed, the entire bar is rocking
to his final note; one you would have snickered at another
day. He did not sing to the young girls, their smeared pouts,
because your lips are staffed with ballads he will never write.

You knew it would end this way: a ditty slurred into a hymn
on a paper napkin, fake numbers stumbled
across a ripped matchbook, fingers bruised
with the ache of wanting. Desire's laugh is ironic.

A guy leaves a bar, a guitar strapped to his back.
You watch him go: a swallow of gin down the drain
when you most need a drink, a song remembered
swelling in your throat, a punchline lost in your head.

Breaking In

Driving your car
in the pouring rain
pavement slicks behind
me like deadly taffy,
like eyeless oceans. Bright
looking-glass of fate
the headlight of your motorcycle
in the rearview mirror
a steady beam, a moon
galloping into the night
where I wait: my heart
a feral horse, my heart,
a two-lane road
you own without raingear
in a thunderstorm. For hours
I can't feel your wet skin,
your shivers along my flank,
my eyes roll behind
and ahead. Wet leaves,
slipping tires, flash of lightning
hooves cutting across the black storm.
Your bike a solid, rust-less sound
that breaks open my body
herding me into this last run
down a road where we will drown,
strip down or grow old; my heart
a blaring horn, my heart a rumble
of flesh, my heart — I know better
than to love you this much — and I swear,
I swear on this velvet sky, on this
squalling stampede I will hold you
always like a horse holds sunlight running,
like untamed bones, like breath.

I'm Sure You Were Handsome

If I saw you tomorrow would I remember
your whiskey-eyed guile? I recall my beer bottle
held by the neck, the slippery glass beaded
with sweat; maybe you wondered if your hand fit
just as perfectly around mine, its heart-shaped palm
strangely uncalloused but rough enough
to silence a gasp.

Fueled by a fumbled football,
hatred for a mother whose soft moans
were heard weeknights through cracks
in sheetrock between rooms, and the men
hidden behind locked doors and fluorescent smiles;
or maybe my slumped shoulders signified
a sickness you thought could be cured.

Prayer was a silent monk struggling with celibacy,
so I counted instead, my dizzy head subtracted
the seconds it took for you to find my zipper
from the number of times I swiveled my hips
away, multiplied by how many
red beer cups were stacked in the corner you stood
all night gunning down each skirted smile with charm;
I calculated sleep would save me soon.

After you slid from me like skin from a snake,
rolled off to the side of the bed, I dreamt
of Leda, her limp body curled around mine,
pale white feathers comforting us, *a strange
heart beating where it lies.*

If you were a swan, I'd recognize you
anywhere – nesting calmly near lakes I won't swim,
brooding over your wedge with a clear eye,
stalking fish you can't eat like a god.

Camouflage

A hunted animal communicates
better than the hunter, a man who only listens
for a certain crackle in the forest of his mind,
can hear a deer snort a mile upwind, but can't
identify a heartbeat in the fingertips of a woman.

Lawn scattered with animal carcasses in various
degrees of decay, hearts eaten by the kind of wolf
only known in midnight's howlings, you're guided
by a moon unable to sympathize with animal pain
for she has given birth to too much joy.

The rage this causes stalks you, bites at your fingertips
like the raccoon you tried to tame one summer who
left you with a houseful of trash and a litter of helpless
little angers you had no idea how to feed.

So when you start listing the three things a woman
is good for, I stop listening, think of a tenderness
only heard once: the night your truck smashed into
a hulk of bear and it whimpered

a story more painful than its broken back;
a tale you could never track like a coyote
in a snowstorm, yielding to your fingertips, a woman's
surrender, with one last, lonely cry.

What You Came For

I try not to imagine how you felt the night
you burst through my front door bellowing
days after our break up, IPA-fueled, poison-
filled boar, claiming love, a hollowed rot,
a kicked paper nest, the pests rising in fury.

Always ignored, boundaries rubbed down to nubs,
you unhinged locked doors, left windowpanes shattered,
the aftermath of a natural disaster —
tornadoes have manners, their wreckage stunning
in early evening — but you

you were a stampede swallowing bystanders, dust-devils
licking your heels, storming through the last bit of light
to kick a dead love's carcass. You, with your fists full
of wasps, mouth a cavern of howls —
hoped to declaw vultures picking my guts,

hoped to wring the jackal's neck —
stomp upstairs where I stand in my panties,
a resurrection of bones threaded with lace,
Singed wings spreading, a fearless singing
opening my throat. You cast me aside,

eyes finally wide open as the bedroom door.
When the man standing behind me turns around
the wasps whisper silent, your mouth closes, an empty
field dark with pig's blood, your feet leading the hearse
back through the damage, your exit a shallow grave.

Morning Light

I remember that first morning love,
alarms silenced in veiled sunlight,
murmuring in half-sleep, twisted together.

We were thieves resting unsaddled and weary
from too much running, my hips heavy
unpredicted rain, the stones of time slowing

the rushed river, your mouth and hands
robbing the overflow, mapping a new course.
Unmasked finally, our skin

brilliant and slaked, buzzed with a
fine glint like matches striking
and striking again just before the flare.

Your body was a welcomed weight,
no longer armed with darkness
a wild approval moved me,

a wild chance found this warm
beast galloping suddenly in our chests,
cave angels escaped from howling,

hushed in a blur of earned tenderness —
the last word of an echo whispered
through a valley of bandits dead from desire.

Our faces recognize each other this close,
rebel light uncloaked, kidnapped stars bursting
into morning for the first time, every time.

Desire

I want you breathless, hoarse whisper
of your throat, a gasp down my back,

I want you awake to my skin,
slick scales sliding through fingers,

my skin your only cover from every hell
that awaits you, the burn you couldn't turn

away. I want you greedy
as both hands, greedy as again:

rivers rioting through cities, carnivores
sniffing the air. I want fires that forests could never name,

hot gingerroot in bathwater, smooth, sunning stones,
hot as stings from a smoking hive,

fingers reaching. I want you aching
like too much, like never enough,

I want you tongue and skin and sweat without sheets,
without mattress, without bed

because none could hold this,
not this perfect swallow slowly arcing,

wings braced for the plunge.

Lost Men

They come to me, fists full of rain,
daisy petals crushed in motorcycle helmets,
faces bewildered, eyes empty wells.

They appear on my doorstep, torsos
dipped in Apollo's gold, bruises
from fastballs and hockey pucks flowering

their bodies, black eyes
wet with creek water, the perfect rock
heavy in their hand.

They show up at the bar, smiles
crooked borders erasing,
remind me of lives they didn't live,

disappear before their favorite songs
shake the jukebox: offerings.
They slide sports cars into close spaces,

scratch vague notes on my windshield, the mirror.
They come to me asking, they come to me begging,
they come to me smelling

of heavy machinery and last night's dreams,
my breath on their neck their first waking thought.
They come to me aching like muscles

shoveling graves, stack beating hearts
like misbehaved woodpiles,
angry (they don't know why they are here)

their shoulders unpack wishes,
unused parachutes,
heads slowly turn for my answer.

They come to me, muddy hands,
dusty words picked from the side of the road,
arrange their questions on the smooth bar,

edit with calloused fingers, search
this unguarded map, the untethered stars,
for a way to get home.

IV

On Being Grown-Up

We know better. Our cautiously casual
conversations, awkward hugs prove we've reached
the handshake of adulthood. Nothing unusual
about turning a cheek to be kissed by a cheek.

Old friends at dinner parties clink glasses, don't wink, each
knows what to hide from a spouse. Cautiously casual
hugs barely count as embrace, time teaches
us the quiet handshake of adulthood. Not unusual

when the ticks of settled passions dig into the guts of
old friends at dinner parties. Clink glasses, don't wink, each
old story has awkward moments we try to twist shut.
Hugs barely count as embrace. Time doesn't teach

to forget slow dances in garages, kisses in laundry rooms.
When the ticks of settled passions dig into my guts
they swell there like the discomfort of silence. Assume
old stories will have awkward moments, new twists develop:

(slow-motion sex in garages, forgotten kisses in barrooms)
cryptic conversations, awkward hugs prove we've reached
in, but are unable to mine those glutted memories. They bloom.
I turn a cheek to be kissed by a cheek.

The Trick

The jilted lover
lingers at her door
without knocking
She prays he vanish
disappear like a botched
magic trick
so the awkwardness might pass
so she can release
the doves from the pit of her stomach
But dead roses
keep appearing out of air so thin
she can't breathe
The slaughtered rabbit's
blood pools in her hat
What will it take to sever
this relationship she asks
lying down in the wooden box
like a distressed assistant
the saw moving magically
on its own.

This Ruined World

Something whispers just below
the surface but we are nearly catatonic
and the well is deeper than all we wish
to fling into it. Buckets lowered
bear everything we hold dear, nothing we hold
dear, our thirst hauled up
to wet numb lips.

We imagine sunken bodies, the bones
of old rivers and older men, eyes black
with dying. Small curved questions
swirl near the surface: the women.

We want so much the water is exhausted,
the well is sick of giving, nobody
is quenched. Finally, when the water opens
its mouth, the world surges out:
hunger, sea glass, the moon's roar,
tender hands, riots; the last few tears
splash the surface like dropped stars.
And don't forget the stones holding their breath
waiting for us to wake up
and drown; the heavy heavy
stones.

.

Philter

While you sleep I dream of cauldrons;
each night a different stone
heats a new belly. Your eyelash
on my pillow beckons my private moon.
I dig through laundry, your missing
button is lost in washers that don't exist.
I am not mad: lizard eyes and wolfbane
can't be found on short notice, and
I don't believe in forcing some
body to love. I can stand missing you
when we part; that thick sludge
of solitude pacifies my tongue,
slicks my thighs — possessing
is weakness I can't abide.

When I bottle your smell —
an attic cupboard afghan frayed
with too much holding, grass stained
with dark engine oil, the last sigh
of whiskey on summer's breath,
an oyster mushroom just harvested,
soil still clinging to stem — it's a reminder
of loss not yet imagined. This shredded ginseng
root, drop of river water, this heavy honeydew
flesh is not lure. The wild I cannot hold
could slip down my throat like the last sip
of everything you ever offered.
I dream of magic; the art of bind
and release, the secret science of forage
and preserve petrifies amber
slivers I hide in the space behind my teeth.
Ancient languages seize my mouth,
fistfuls of spells empty into the dark.

Summer Night

It's a summer night just bright enough to put you to rest. Stars
point like tiny teeth in somebody else's mouth. Test stars

on another visit, learn to understand a language no god discerns,
silence the drunk singing in the background, swivel into a gesture stars

recognize on their own: a nod, an inhale, eyeing upward.
You slam your car door, look up and from your chest, stars

erupt. Shrapnel you've kept hidden in your heart's pocket, sizeable chunks
require unaffordable surgery, so you dig in your fingernails, an almost caress.
    Stars

hide another body, carpet over the blood black sky with their shining, flash
    lights flicker
in a dark field blot out your sigh, the air in your mouth compressed stars.

Listen. I heard your heart stop way over here, Love, the light arrived faster.
I'm sorry I didn't look up in time, that small sound, an *oh*, consumed by a
    nest of stars.

Don't Take My Advice

Write about something else; you aren't that interesting, I tell
my students, but don't take my own advice. I write about

my wilderness, my son, my Catskill town where the best stories
come from trees and gin mills. I want to write about politics,

humpback whales, Korea and churches. But I can't divine holiness
in monsters that eat worlds raw, machines that spin gears around oily

surfaces, slick with the knowing of once-wise men. I am overwhelmed
by oceans and foreign languages. Where are the haughty poems –

Agamemnon dragging your mind through the Trojan dust? Where is
the boldness that sent Whitman yawping over tenement houses and shacks?

What about the questions that sent St. Paul to Damascus, Ginsberg
to the crazy house? Maybe you believe

in the power of gods, drugs or heroes. That has nothing to do with what
kind of poem you will write. Or maybe it does, because today I'm thinking

about Cupid's disobedience, the smoky afterthought of a good buzz,
the burnt skull and love letters of an American boy in Iraq, and my mind

detonates like a car bomb: No, it's safer to write about my infant son's
wrinkled palms, my small town's moldy bars, lilacs, and my miles and miles

of misty woods, wild with the growth of understanding, infested
with dangling caterpillars, holding onto their world like a question.

These Days

These days the rain won't quit. The sky dumps itself empty
until all that's left are shuddering sighs. Your car's rusted muffler
scrapes the pavement, and in the rearview it sits in the middle of the road
like an abandoned hitchhiker extending a middle finger.

Your kids are hungry and there's only peanut butter and crackers in the cupboard.
The refrigerator door groans revealing a coffin-like staleness.
Your last ten bucks buys a pack of smokes even though you quit
three years ago. Your shoulders are frozen in a permanent shrug.
You don't answer the phone — bill collectors are casing your house
while the dogs turn their heads and pant at the smell of greed. Last week,

there were three burglaries on this street, but you don't fix the broken locks;
the unlatched screen door reminds you of the wind, its steady bumping
a nagging ghost. You haven't forgotten your grandmother's rough laugh,
rougher hands that braided your hair so tight your scalp cried; those hands that
smacked the sense right back into you. You haven't forgotten. You haven't
    forgotten the rain.

But you also haven't forgotten the sun: the children across the way stomp
in puddles, the car's engine turns over, still eager to take you where
you need to go. Your grandmother's clear eyes were full of the devil
and the wisdom to beat him senseless. You laugh. The mass of daffodils
by your porch-stoop raise their heads, yellow smiles resurrect dreams,
look for the light even in that gray expanse of sky.

Early Spring, Sullivan County, NY

Early morning a woman's dog sniffs individual blades of grass, the sun rises
over the reservoir while they hike, orange and purple childhood watercolors drizzle
into the gray basin. Sudsy snow melts around sharp green daffodil shoots
fighting like knives for the light. A neighbor's goat runs to the fence,
speaks softly in greeting, dainty as a Victorian maiden, and the pussy willows
weep ice in the warming ditches. Across the valley,

a small town yawns: cars loiter at gas station pumps. Women in unbuttoned coats
wrestle with nozzles, as men, mud-smeared jeans faded at the seams, hoist
themselves into pick-up trucks, thick coffee spilling from Styrofoam cups.
A restaurant owner turns his key, nods to the teenager crossing the street,
headphones blaring Kaine X Bleek, the rhythm moving him, mesmerized
bronze liquid, to the corner barbershop. A few miles away, young boys play tag

behind wire fences, their shouts a cacophony of little prayers, mothers
tending babies whisper at picnic tables. Here, the Delaware River nudges
its banks, here, the mountain trails meander
in mist, here the tourist takes a selfie at the corner of Hurd and West Shore,
lights a joint and passes it to the long-haired stranger to his left. At the college,
two girls walk arm in arm, their smiles unscripted songs; a boy bounces
a basketball on a wet court. Driving Route 17,

you roll down your window, inhale the wet litany of spring, the Bashakill spreading
before you, a quivering dream unscarred by wreckage, rusty hinges, car tires.
In a tavern, a bartender watches the musician's fingers position on guitar frets,
his voice a sultry cocktail. Jutting from mountainsides, ghosts of hotels, windows
like broken teeth, cement a solitude only known by abandonment. I sit
on a rotting porch chair, watch an eagle circle while down the hill

a fisherman shivers in his waders, casts his fly, the trout forever looking upstream,
the water welcoming him home.

When Sadness Comes

> "There is nothing I can do
> against your coming.
> *When I awake, I am still with thee.*"
>
> —Jane Kenyon, "Having It Out With Melancholy"

He hovers over your bed, snatches the morning sunshine and sticks it in his pipe.

He croons, be my guest, and bends to blow the *bile of desolation* into your lungs.

You avoid his stare, look at the blank wall instead; it offers no advice.

The room holds its breath. You break the silence with a muffled sob.

Sadness does not offer you a tissue.

Guilt drops by, puts her arm around his shoulder, nudges your body like you would a sleeping cat.

You turn over, use the pillow to shield her eyes, but she shoves you, grabs the pillow, demands your attention. Guilt is the mother of all feelings.

Sadness tips his hat, takes a step back.

You slink out of bed, force your feet to move you to the kitchen for coffee, to the closet for clothes.

Sadness smiles slowly like a saxophone player, says

I'll be here all day.

Slipstream

After the rain, minnows wriggle
To the surface, silver lilt
Of starlight tinning through water.
How do they know this is happiness?
Their smiles undetected wink open
Sacrificing each breath to gulp, a hunger
Mistaken for panic. A poison-less dart
Avoids my trailing hand, a light wrinkle
In chaos when you appear:
ghost of a scar I vaguely detect
But want to explain nonetheless,
A weeping tattoo fishtails down
My torso. Pearly clouds build
In the wake of this galaxy, your memory
Drowns the small, swimming stars,
Their bliss, you once said,
An opening wound, a free choice, surrender.

What the Truth is Worth

These are not confessions, they are bone
               bled truths,
                         they are words trapped
                         in marrow that burn you
                         alive if left unsaid.
       They are barn-burners, house-wreckers, black
cigarette holes left in your mom's new couch
               after nodding out.

They are dog-stranglers, son-smackers,   the car flipped
                                              in a field as
                                      you flee,
                  a bleeding child in your arms.

They are infidelity held in your mouth,
                                 a sour tongue,
the girl hit, closed fisted, in tenth grade homeroom.

Shame's clenched jaws keep secrets   for most,
               but don't believe
secrets save.

               I'm free with my truths
               so others feel safe to tell theirs.

A wounded world gapes behind the construct
                              of admissible truths
glittering with grime and warped mirrors.   It undulates like knife accidents
               viewed through tears,   begs us to return,
                     beckons in the dreams we wake from alive
gasping, looking around.

               You do not seek relief; you unpack
                                  the bloody lunch,
                                  still twitching, eye
   the unhinged gates of heaven.
                 The almighty absence is a cool breeze
rattling useless latches.
                 You settle into the firepit,
                     cover a blanket of flames,   un-
pray for forgiveness.

It's best, you say, if you keep that opinion between us

When told to be silent, my body goes deaf;
a flatlined squeal flashes red behind my eyes,
my tongue seizes up. The girls I never kissed
goodbye buried inside of me shudder; they
were always the quiet ones, forced to hide truths
to keep monsters safe. Hush me
and my fangs sharpen, I unravel at the seams
in a litany of blood growls. My thorny mouth
thickens with the wildness of zombies
resurrected by a gentle suggestion. They stagger
out, rush into this muddy river of risk that sucks
them under again and again, but they rise
without quit; dark Ophelias who cannot float,
bruised with the safety of silence, the scabbed trigger
picked raw, words unfettered, mouths opening.

Trash Talk

Around here, girls have dirty mouths, tongues like switches we cut ourselves
from the bleeding trees in the backyard – nobody has to beat us, we know
we did wrong. Around here dirt covers our names like the backroads we run,
the woods are deep enough to hide a body, and my body always wants to be
    hidden.

The bleeding trees in the backyard have beat us, we know
when mama goes out for milk, she'll comes back with a heroin problem.
The woods are deep enough to hide a body, my body always wants to be hidden
behind the woodpile where smoke from the firepit seasons my hair.

When mama goes out for milk, she'll come back with heroin — only a problem
if you make it one. The cold spring is cracking our pipes but around here
the woodpile is where we smoke, ashes from the firepit season my hair.
We heft hammers, walk without stuttering, the splinters in our throats a mercy

if you make it one. The cold spring is cracking our pipes but around here
our short skirts are no invitation, and if we are hungry enough, we'll fix anything.
We heft hammers, walk without stuttering, the splinters in our throats a mercy
from the weight in our stomachs blossomed from apple seeds we refused to spit.

Don't act like you didn't know how this story ends, our bellies are deep, we know
we did wrong. Dirt covers our names. Like the backroads, we run
farther into the woods but always end up sitting on our own front porch.
Around here, girls have dirty mouths, tongues like switches we cut ourselves.

These Boots Were Made

When choosing a route through a thicket
Always follow deer runs, trails
Grooved by hooves and antlers, muscles and teeth.
Boot prints mislead the bigger and deeper
They sink into mud: even boots
Themselves, polite, lined up on the porch, mud
Caked on the worn leather, laces tucked,
Sleep through the stomp echoing down
Long wooden hallways women have swept
Clean, scrubbed on hands and knees, mouths
Quiet and splintered. Listen: the women
On their knees never pray, never beg
God for the hassle, we are practicing
Being born. Our silence is not submission,
Ears tuned to the animals moving in our bodies,
Looking for paths boots haven't marked,
Trails that lead out of our skin, down branching corridors,
Past those soldiers on the front porch, silent
Through fields and thickets. The thrashing
Of our bones leads us away from ourselves, away
From the hollow structures where we slept
Like threadbare tapestries, our skin spread above
Mantels, crackle of dry leaves behind
Our teeth. Glass eyes blink back at the frantic
Boot prints circling vacant spaces,
Grass rustles with our disappearing.

.

Re-Vision

> "Out of the ash
> I rise with my red hair
> And I eat men like air."
>
> —Sylvia Plath, "Lady Lazarus"

The god has arranged for my daughter, my mother, my sisters
and a mouthful of broken teeth. He has invoked historical accuracy.
There are angels in the paintings chipping away the devil
until his scales bleed, until our nails scratch out the sky.
Nobody believes women. Nobody believes women
in danger. Dig us up; the moon casts
new shadows as we catch breath. Please, we begged then, please, we practiced
our speeches. Ropes burned our tongues. Everybody clapped. Everybody
   believes women
are dangerous; we will dye our bridal gowns red, birth
fires that can't be contained in our heads. Savage blazes, museums of ash,
   smoking
cathedrals — god,
you want to fuck with us? You want us to say we feel free?
We don't choke on the air we eat.
You thought we were carrion, but our mouths are full of fur, our thighs
full of sky.
We are the birds circling, circling.

The River Knows

The river knows my name. The river gulps down my shame
Like her mouth is on fire, like the flames could lick her

At a drinking game. The river sleeps beside me, forgets to get up
And leave, doesn't give me a reason. She keeps her bones to herself,

But offers her hidden bodies like prizes I want to win, the carnival of ghosts
Sliding off the pines and boulders where I grow my stories.

The river listens for the warning bell,
Pretends she didn't feel the storm coming, didn't notice the fishing boats

Pulling up anchors and heading home, fish circling my legs like a dance.
The river smells my mountain hair, rears up like a welt, like I don't

Belong so close, my throat slick with the ginseng on my breath
A dead giveaway. The river stands in my way, says *find a new path*, so I get out
   my shovel,

Dig up that mongrel always hot on my trail, its breath cool as distant snow
   at my neck.
The river shrugs when I chuck my compass, chokes on its southwestern

Charm, riots as I wipe my feet at her banks, track the hound's
Pawprints, our feral galloping slaps her clenched jaw. The river

Will not look back, the blue ridge of a memory holds her down, the river
Has a mean side-eye, but keeps it moving, is unable to wave

Goodbye.
.

Circus Life

We run from our names, keep our mouths
sealed shut as back pockets, filthy from use,
always come back to this clapboard town.

The streets all lead to the last point south,
imaginary boundaries loop us in chalk, we refuse
the run of our names, keep our mouths

private as checks we can't cash. We've grown
weary of jukeboxes moaning our names, loose
and musical as change. Coming back to this bloodshot town,

pinpricked pride burns like shots going down;
the trap in trapeze is a pendulum — we don't choose.
We run from our names, keep our mouths

full of calico, colors melting off tongues rough
as the last ride home, a dirt road potholed, abused.
We run from our names, keep our mouths

close to smiling, a barely audible hiss sounds
alarms across the county. Please excuse
us, our names. They run soft in our mouths,
sing us all the way back to the ghost of this town.

Our Only Escape

After we drink the flying
potion, the feathers

inside us won't lie down,
won't be still, our blood tricked

with the dream
breeze singing through stars —

light reaches places words
can't touch, the dark skies, wombs

where we hide scars and poppies,
oceans, mirrors. The authors

of men and angels swell
with failure, unable to quell tongues,

venom. Our daughters need more
protection from the hell of blooming.

We gather the wings of flightless
birds, wrap them around valerian root,

concoct a tincture to purge the wax of silence
softly from our skin. A skein of forgetting unknotted,

we head out in no particular direction
leaving men on the ground blind, voiceless,

wandering in circles.

Small Town Prayers

In the moment of white shining
we forget what we are.

We forget that we called them,
though not to be saved.

The stars are far from this town
but the sky remembers their brightness.

There is nothing beautiful here,
but there are small fish in the creek,

a crumbling fountain enclosed
by benches, Harleys idling in the husky lull

of dusk's Main Street, basking in
the thick of breath we forgot to hold

just before the blessing.
A rush of air swallows us,

then stillness.
The hush of angels crashes out of the night.

August Light

> "And that was all that meant, just that luminous lambent quality of an older light than ours."
>
> —William Faulkner

If you can smell the Four Roses on my breath, you are not paying attention: the fields are bleached to bone, days are quiet as storm-forced reckoning. The trees don't move an inch, hold their breath, hold their own, hold the last bit of green summer will allow before it moans into the next death. We are dying and don't even know it; the maw of the beast so ordinary we forget it's there waiting for us to sleep through another heartbreak. I wouldn't know a crocus if I saw it because this light is holding me steady, is yellowing the corners of old photos in my mind —

childhood summers when the ground dusted bare feet with skeletons of dead flowers; running through fields, my child's body disappears, my mother's worry another land I haven't set foot in since her mother is still alive waving from the back yard, her fingers dark from unearthing new ways to keep the past where it lies. What does it mean when you call your ancestors from graves you didn't dig and adulthood forces you to search for the roots in another

soil? I miss the teeth in the smile my grandmother lost; the front porch she sat on for years on a mountain I can't name sags, invites me home. Catskill light falls at summer's end same as Blue Ridge light, but the mountains, the mountains here don't recognize my breath, the dark whiskey that colors it. That light is older than everything I know, that light will bathe me, put me to bed, bury me where I belong.

Acknowledgments

Grateful acknowledgments to the editors of the following journals, magazines and anthologies in which these poems first appeared published under the name Lisa Caloro:

3Elements: "Circus Life"
Cactus Heart: "After Ever"
Cloud of Possibility: "Things I Don't Tell My Children" and "What We Believe"
The Cape Rock: "Ride it Out"
The Carolina Quarterly: "Lost Men"
The Chaffey Review: "Night Fishing"
Chronogram: "So The Story Goes" and "When Sadness Comes"
Dying Dahlia Review: "Things I Tell My Children"
The Evening Review: "Vision"
Green Door Magazine: "All In"
Harpur Palate: "Camouflage"
Jelly Bucket: "A Woman Wants to Make Love to a Poet;" "It's best, you say, if you keep that opinion between us;" "When Not Hungry, Restless"
Kaaterskill Basin Literary Journal: "Don't Take My Advice" and "Small Town Prayers"
Madcap: "Over Shots of Tequila You Ask What My Bee Poem Means and Why I Always Push You Off the Cliff in Your Dream" and "Our Only Escape"
The Packingtown Review: "What the Truth is Worth" and "God's Reply"
Painted Bride Quarterly: "Summer Night"
The Penn Review: "Lost Art"
Santa Ana River Review: "Midnight Hives"
Slant: "Even gods"
Slipstream: "Eve's First Party"
Stone Canoe: "Breaking In"
Sullivan Allies Leading Together: "These Days"
SUPLA: "Early Spring, Sullivan County, NY"
Vanguard Voices of the Hudson Valley: "Clarity"

Thank you to Louisa Lam, Shannon Bainsky, and Gabe Rikard for reading crappy drafts, editing, assuaging my anxiety, and for always cheering the loudest.

Thank you to Lynne Crockett and Jason Irwin for reading my manuscript and giving me essential feedback.

Special thanks to Vern Lindquist who read all of these poems multiple times over many years, and who was never afraid to tell me things like "the word pelvis should never appear in a poem." This book wouldn't exist without him and his wife, Lisa, who is an actual angel.

Thank you to the DVAA and Sullivan County Libraries for recognizing me and selecting me to be the Second Poet Laureate of Sullivan County, NY.

Thank you to the essential artists in my life, and their vision: Anne Marchal, Dara Perlman, and Jeff Prybolsky.

To my family: I love you.

Endless love and appreciation to my bar family, especially Wade St. Germain and RJ Baker, but also Tammy and Billy and Mikey and Corey and BJ and Dave and Mike B and Mike M and Eli and Jay and Deb and Anne-Marie and Neil and Donny and Kate and Julie and the rest of the Cab Frank's crew for accepting me at my messiest and most fierce, for allowing me to be the voices in these poems without shame, and for saying "Love you" as I kicked them out the door. Thank you to the rest of my small-town industry folks for the buy-backs and small mercies. Y'all called me a poet, and it was so.

Thank you to my children, Sarah and Nicholas, for being the reason I draw in air and spit out words.

About the Author

Lisa Titus (formerly Lisa Caloro) tends bar and teaches college in a small Catskill Mountain town. She was the 2020-2021 Poet Laureate of Sullivan County, NY; the recipient of a 2021-2022 DVAA Individual Artist Fellowship; and a 2020 Pushcart Prize nominee. Her poems have appeared in *Barrow Street*, *The Carolina Quarterly*, *The Packingtown Review*, and elsewhere. She lives in Sullivan County, New York.

Our Mission

The mission of Brick Road Poetry Press is to publish and promote poetry that entertains, amuses, edifies, and surprises a wide audience of appreciative readers. We are not qualified to judge who deserves to be published, so we concentrate on publishing what we enjoy. Our preference is for poetry geared toward dramatizing the human experience in language rich with sensory image and metaphor, recognizing that poetry can be, at one and the same time, both familiar as the perspiration of daily labor and as outrageous as a carnival sideshow

Available from Brick Road Poetry Press

www.brickroadpoetrypress.com

All These Hungers by Rick Mulkey
Escape Envy by Ace Boggess
My Father Should Die in Winter by Barry Marks
The Return of the Naked Man by Robert Tremmel
Reading Szymborska in a Time of Plague by Joan Baranow

Available from Brick Road Poetry Press

www.brickroadpoetrypress.com

The Word in Edgewise by Sean M. Conrey
Household Inventory by Connie Jordan Green
Practice by Richard M. Berlin
A Meal Like That by Albert Garcia
Cracker Sonnets by Amy Wright
Things Seen by Joseph Stanton
Battle Sleep by Shannon Tate Jonas
Lauren Bacall Shares a Limousine by Susan J. Erickson
Ambushing Water by Danielle Hanson
Having and Keeping by David Watts
Assisted Living by Erin Murphy
Credo by Steve McDonald
The Deer's Bandanna by David Oates
Creation Story by Steven Owen Shields
Touring the Shadow Factory by Gary Stein
American Mythology by Raphael Kosek
Waxing the Dents by Daniel Edward Moore
Speaking Parts by Beth Ruscio
Ultra Deep Field by Ace Boggess
Secret Formulas & Techniques of the Masters by Jackie Craven
Thrash by Michael Diebert
Face Cut Out For Locket by Jenn Blair
Natural Violence By Jennifer Brown
Miracle Strip by Matthew Layne
The Prisoners by Ace Boggess
Eulogy for an Imperfect Man by Maureen A. Sherbondy

Also Available from Brick Road Poetry Press

www.brickroadpoetrypress.com

Dancing on the Rim by Clela Reed
Possible Crocodiles by Barry Marks
Pain Diary by Joseph D. Reich
Otherness by M. Ayodele Heath
Drunken Robins by David Oates
Damnatio Memoriae by Michael Meyerhofer
Lotus Buffet by Rupert Fike
The Melancholy MBA by Richard Donnelly
Two-Star General by Grey Held
Chosen by Toni Thomas
Etch and Blur by Jamie Thomas
Water-Rites by Ann E. Michael
Bad Behavior by Michael Steffen
Tracing the Lines by Susanna Lang
Rising to the Rim by Carol Tyx
Treading Water with God by Veronica Badowski
Rich Man's Son by Ron Self
Just Drive by Robert Cooperman
The Alp at the End of My Street by Gary Leising

www.ingramcontent.com/pod-product-compliance
Lightning Source LLC
Chambersburg PA
CBHW021020090426
42738CB00007B/843